Easy Recipes for Cat Biscuits

Tasty Biscuits That Your Feline Friend Will Love

BY: Valeria Ray

License Notes

Copyright © 2021 Valeria Ray All Rights Reserved

All rights to the content of this book are reserved by the Author without exception unless permission is given stating otherwise.

The Author have no claims as to the authenticity of the content and the Reader bears all responsibility and risk when following the content. The Author is not liable for any reparations, damages, accidents, injuries or other incidents occurring from the Reader following all or part of this publication.

Table of Contents

Introduction 5

    Homemade biscuits 7

    Cheddar cat biscuits 9

    Salmon cat biscuits 11

    Pumpkin cat biscuits 13

    Quick cat biscuits 15

    Cheesy cat biscuits 17

    Sweet potato cat biscuits 19

    Soft cat biscuits 21

    Simple cat biscuits 23

    Oat cat biscuits 25

    Cranberry chicken cat biscuits 27

    Quinoa flour cat biscuits 29

    Natural cat biscuits 31

    Coconut oil cat biscuits 33

    Turkey catnip cat biscuits 35

Valentine's day cat biscuits 37

Chewy cat biscuits 39

Tuna cat biscuits 41

Nutritional cat biscuits 43

Parmesan cat biscuits 45

Apple sauce cat biscuits 47

Bacon Cat treats 49

Birthday cat treat 51

Cheese cat biscuits 53

Chicken yogurt cat biscuits 55

Tuna oat cat biscuits 57

Cat biscuits from cat food 59

Budget cat biscuits 61

Turkey cat biscuits 63

Easy home cooked cat biscuits 65

Conclusion 67

About the Author 68

Author's Afterthoughts 69

Introduction

Cooking biscuits for your pet can be a fun process. The Cat biscuit recipe book makes it easy for you to make healthy treats with a few ingredients that you already have at home. Each recipe has carefully chosen ingredients to provide your cat with the proper nutrients for good health. If your cat suffers from allergies, homemade food is the best choice. You get to control the ingredients, choosing only whole foods free of artificial flavors.

Cats with dietary sensitivities will benefit from homemade biscuits. When you control the ingredients, you can avoid the common food allergens for cats. The preparation is straightforward, as you only need to toss a few ingredients, make a dough, and shape the biscuits. It is quick and clear, so you don't need to spend much of your time.

Are you ready to discover healthy cat biscuit recipes and provide your furry friend with wholesome nutrients? Let's go through the cat biscuit recipes!

Homemade biscuits

Cooking tasty treats for your kitty is now simple and easy. Within half an hour, you can prepare 40 crunchy treats for your feline friend. Your cat will love this healthy and tasty treat that you have prepared with love and joy.

Time: 30 minutes

Yields: 40

Ingredients

- 1 can tuna in oil, drained
- 1 ¼ cups of flour
- 1 egg
- 1 teaspoon parsley
- ½ cup water

Instructions

Set the oven to 350.

Add the flour, tuna, egg, parsley, and water to a food processor.

If the dough seems sticky, adjust with a bit of flour.

Sprinkle the working surface with flour and roll out the dough to half-inch thickness.

Cut out with small cookie cutters to your liking.

Arrange a sheet pan with baking paper and place the biscuits. Bake your cat biscuits for 20 minutes and let them cool after removing.

Cheddar cat biscuits

The combination of cheddar and tuna is a perfect gourmet treat for your cat. If you feel like your cat doesn't like tuna, you can always switch it to salmon or chicken. We understand that some cats are picky eaters, so feel free to modify the recipe as needed.

Time: 30 minutes

Yields: 40

Ingredients

- 1 can tuna packed in water, drained
- 1 egg
- 1/3 cup shredded cheddar cheese
- 1 tablespoon dried catnip
- 1 1/3 cups oat flour
- 1/2 cup cold water

Instructions

Arrange a sheet pan with baking paper.

Add the cheese and tuna to a food processor and pulse. Add the catnip, egg, and oat flour. Pulse to combine.

Add the cold water gradually until it shapes into a dough ball.

Divide the cat biscuit dough into four pieces and wrap them with plastic wrap.

Let the cat biscuit dough cool in the fridge for half an hour.

Set the oven to 350.

Sprinkle the working surface with flour and shape it into a long stick. Chop into small chunks and roll to balls. Press with a form to flatten.

Stack onto the baking sheet and bake for ten to 15 minutes.

Salmon cat biscuits

With only three ingredients, you can prepare the best treats for your cat. The simple process reveals how to cook them and have your treats ready for the next two weeks.

Time: 40 minutes

Yields: 40

Ingredients

- 1 egg beaten
- 10 oz. canned salmon
- 2 cups whole wheat flour

Instructions

Set the oven to 350.

Bring the oats to your food processor and pulse to grind.

Mix the salmon, flour, and beaten egg in the bowl of a stand mixer. Turn it on and make a dough. Add a little water in case the biscuit dough is too dry.

Sprinkle the working surface with flour and roll out the dough.

Cut out with small cookie cutters to your liking.

Arrange a sheet pan with baking paper and place the biscuits. Bake the cat biscuits for 20 minutes and let them cool after removing.

Pumpkin cat biscuits

The combination of natural ingredients provides healthy treats with an abundance of nutrients. Prepare a large batch and store it for the upcoming week.

Time: 35 minutes

Yields: 20

Ingredients

- 1 (4 oz) can of salmon packed in water, unsalted
- 1 egg
- 1/3 cup pumpkin puree
- 1/2 cup old fashioned oats
- 2 tablespoons avocado oil

Instructions

Set the oven to 325.

Add your old-fashioned oats to a food processor and blend into flour.

Drain the canned salmon.

Mix the salmon, pumpkin, oat flour, avocado, and egg. Shape the dough into tiny biscuits.

Line a baking sheet with paper and place the biscuits. Bake for 25 minutes and let them cool after removing.

Quick cat biscuits

The secret trick to preparing delicious cat treats is to add a dash of catnip. Your kitties will love this fantastic recipe, but you will also enjoy repairing it.

Time: 35 minutes

Yields: 25

Ingredients

- 1 egg
- 1 tablespoon catnip
- 2 tablespoon extra-virgin olive oil
- 1 cup old fashioned oats
- 1/2 cup pureed turkey

Instructions

Set the oven to 350.

Bring the oats in a food processor and blend into flour.

Add egg, meat, olive oil, and catnip. Process until combined.

Add the mixture into a ziplock bag and cut the corner. Pipe onto a baking sheet lined with baking paper and bake for 10 minutes. Let them cool after removing.

Cheesy cat biscuits

The combination of cheese, yogurt, and whole wheat flour is an excellent gourmet treat for cats. Prepare these cat biscuits and let your pet enjoy a healthy treat when they are behaving well.

Time: 35 minutes

Yields: 60

Ingredients

- 3/4 cup shredded cheddar cheese
- 1/4 cup yogurt, plain
- 3/4 cup whole wheat flour
- A few tablespoons of water
- 5 tablespoons grated Parmesan cheese
- 1/4 cup cornmeal

Instructions

Set the oven to 350. Arrange a sheet pan with baking paper.

Combine the cat biscuit ingredients into a mixing bowl until you have a dough. If the biscuit dough is too dry, add water gradually.

Sprinkle the working surface with flour and roll out the dough to ¼ inch thick. Use a knife to cut ½ inch cubes. Arrange a sheet pan with baking paper and place the biscuits. Bake for 20 minutes and let them cool after removing.

Sweet potato cat biscuits

The soft and chewy salmon treats are perfect for cats that have trouble chewing. If you have an older cat or cat with teeth issues, this is an ideal recipe.

Time: 3 hours 10 minutes

Yields: 35

Ingredients

- 1 can wild-caught salmon
- 1 1/2 cups old-fashioned oats
- 1 1/2 cups sweet potato, baked and mashed
- 1/4 cup fresh parsley

Instructions

Add the sweet potato and salmon to a mixing bowl. Mash them with a fork and mix to combine.

Add the oat and parsley to a food processor and pulse to grind into fine flour.

Transfer the flour mixture to the mixing bowl and combine to make a dough.

Scoop into silicone molds and freeze for two hours.

Soft cat biscuits

These soft treats are a good choice if your cat can't eat crunchy food. Prepare the cheesy soft biscuits with simple ingredients that you already have in your pantry.

Time: 40 minutes

Yields: 24

Ingredients

- 3/4 cup white flour
- 1/4 cup cornmeal
- 1/4 cup plain yogurt
- 5 tablespoons grated Parmesan cheese
- 3/4 cup shredded cheddar cheese

Instructions

Set the oven to 350.

Mix the parmesan, cheddar, and yogurt in a mixing bowl.

Add cornmeal and flour and mix to shape the dough.

Sprinkle the working surface with flour and roll out the dough to ¼ inch thick.

With a knife, cut to one-inch cubes. Arrange a sheet pan with baking paper and place the biscuits. Bake for 20 minutes and leave them to cool after removing.

Simple cat biscuits

With only three simple ingredients, these cat biscuits are a real delicacy. Prepare them within half an hour and let your feline friend enjoy the yumminess.

Time: 30 minutes

Yields: 85

Ingredients

- 1 (3 oz) can of Seafood Classic Pate
- 1 egg
- 1 cup flour

Instructions

Set the oven to 350.

Whisk the egg in a mixing bowl. Add the page and continue to whisk until combined.

Add flour and mix to turn into a dough.

Line the working surface with parchment paper and roll out the dough between two pieces of paper to ¼ inch thick.

Cut out with small cookie cutters to your liking.

Arrange a sheet pan with baking paper and place the biscuits. Bake for 10 minutes and let them cool after removing.

Oat cat biscuits

With only five ingredients, you can make these simple and healthy cat treats. Store them in a cute jar and let your cat enjoy them every day.

Time: 40 minutes

Yields: 40

Ingredients

- ⅔ cup canned tuna, in oil
- 1 tablespoon dried catnip
- 1 egg
- 1 tablespoon olive oil
- 1 cup rice or oat flour

Instructions

Set the oven to 350.

Add flour, tuna, catnip and egg into a mixing bowl. Use a fork to mix until the dough combines. If it appears too dry, add a little olive oil.

Scoop out ½ teaspoon and roll into balls. Place on a paper lined baking sheet and press gently with a spoon to flatten.

Bake for 10 minutes and let them cool after removing.

Cranberry chicken cat biscuits

This recipe shows you how to prepare a large batch of tiny cat treats. Cranberries are approved for cats. However, you need to make sure to include unsweetened ones.

Time: 35 minutes

Yields: 200

Ingredients

- 1 cup rolled oats
- 4 oz. plain chicken, cooked and shredded, without salt
- 3 tablespoons dry cranberries, unsweetened
- 1 heaping tablespoon dried catnip
- 2 tablespoons + 1/2 teaspoon olive oil
- 1 large egg

Instructions

Add the rolled oats to a food processor and process them into fine flour. Add the dry cranberries and process to grind them.

Add the other cat biscuit ingredients and process until combined.

Transfer into a mixing bowl.

Set the oven to 350.

Scoop out ¼ teaspoon of the mixture and shape it into a ball. Press flat with fingers or a spoon.

Line a baking sheet with paper and place the biscuits. Bake for 15 to 17 minutes and let them cool after removing.

Quinoa flour cat biscuits

The healthy cat biscuits are so simple and easy to prepare. All you need to do is toss the ingredient in a food processor and let it do its magic.

Time: 35 minutes

Yields: 50

Ingredients

- ½ cup brown rice flour
- ½ cup quinoa flour
- 4-5 oz sardines
- 1 tablespoon dried catnip
- ¼ cup parsley, rough chopped
- 1 egg
- ½ tablespoon olive oil

Instructions

Set the oven to 350.

Add all the cat biscuit ingredients to a food processor. Pulse to combine into a dough.

Shape the dough into tiny balls. Arrange a sheet pan with parchment paper and place the biscuits. Bake for 10 minutes and let them cool after removing.

Natural cat biscuits

With catnip being cats' favorite, here is another good recipe for aromatic cat biscuits. Feel free to adjust the amount and include one or half a teaspoon in your recipe.

Time: 35 minutes

Yields: 40

Ingredients

- 1-1/2 cups whole wheat flour
- 1/3 cup dry milk
- 1-1/2 teaspoons organic catnip
- 2 tablespoons melted butter
- 1/2 cup milk
- 1 large egg
- 1 tablespoon honey

Instructions

Set the oven to 350.

In a bowl, mix the dry milk, flour, and catnip.

Add the wet ingredients and mix well until dough forms.

Flour the surface and roll out the cat biscuit dough. With a knife, cut small squares, or cut out with small cookie cutters to your liking.

Arrange a sheet pan with baking paper and place the biscuits. Bake for 20 minutes and let them cool after removing.

Coconut oil cat biscuits

With an abundance of healthy nutrients, these coconut oil cookies will do the trick. Your cat will love the tuna and sweet potato combination, enhanced with gelatine.

Time: 40 minutes

Yields: 50

Ingredients

- 2 medium-sized sweet potatoes. mashed
- 1/2 cup of coconut oil
- 1/4 cup of gelatine powder
- 1/2 cup of coconut flour
- 1 egg
- 1 can of tuna, drained

Instructions

In a mixing bowl, combine the cat biscuit ingredients by mashing them. When you reach dough consistency, shape into tiny balls.

Flatten the balls with your fingers or the back of a spoon.

Set the oven to 350.

Arrange a sheet pan with baking paper and place the biscuits. Bake for 20 minutes and let them cool after removing.

Turkey catnip cat biscuits

In case your cat is allergic to grains, this is an excellent recipe to get started. Replace the flour with coconut flour to fit your pet's specific needs.

Time: 40 minutes

Yields: 40

Ingredients

- 1 can of turkey breast
- 1 cup of coconut flour
- 2 tablespoons of coconut oil
- 1 egg
- 1 tablespoon dried catnip
- Water as per requirement

Instructions

Set the oven to 350.

Add the drained canned turkey into your food processor together with the other biscuit ingredients.

Blend until smooth.

Transfer to a working surface and add one tablespoon of water at a time until you reach a nice dough consistency. Cut out with a cookie cutter or into small cubes.

Arrange a sheet pan with baking paper and place the biscuits. Bake the cat treats for 15 minutes and let them cool after removing.

Valentine's day cat biscuits

Even your cat could use some love for valentine's day. Prepare these heart-shaped biscuits and let your pet enjoy the excellent taste.

Time: 50 minutes

Yields: 30

Ingredients

- 1/2-pound chicken breasts
- 1 egg
- 1/4 cup of flour
- 1 tablespoon of catnip
- 1 cup of quick-cooking oats
- 1/3 cup of water

Instructions

Boil the chicken breasts for 20 minutes or till it turns white.

Set the oven to 350.

Add the oats, egg, catnip, and cooked chicken to a food processor. Pulse on low to combine it. Add water gradually to get the consistency of a chicken salad.

Transfer to a bowl and add the flour. Knead into a dough.

Flour the working surface and work the biscuit dough to half-inch thickness.

Cut out with a small heart-shaped cookie cutter.

Arrange a sheet pan with baking paper and place the biscuits. Bake for 20 minutes and let them cool after removing.

Chewy cat biscuits

The secret to preparing this awesome recipe is to use baby food. Since it is already free of artificial ingredients and sweeteners, it is a good fit for your cat's diet.

Time: 40 minutes

Yields: 50

Instructions

- 1 egg
- 2 teaspoons olive oil
- 1 (4 oz) jar chicken and rice baby food
- 1 cup brown rice flour
- 1/4 cup parsley, coarsely chopped
- 1/2 cup cooked rice
- 2 tablespoons water

Instructions

Set the oven to 325. Arrange a sheet pan with baking paper.

Combine the baby food, egg, oil, water, and parsley. Add the cooked rice and mix well.

Spread onto the baking sheet into a rectangle with ⅓ inch thickness. Bake for 15 minutes and let it cool down until you can touch it.

Chop into small pieces enough for your cat to eat.

Bake the chunks for eight minutes and allow them to cool completely.

Tuna cat biscuits

The tuna flour and egg recipe are too simple and easy. Even if you don't have good cooking skills, you can prepare the best cat gourmet biscuits in only 40 minutes. Coconut flour is a perfect replacement for cats that are allergic to grains.

Time: 40 minutes

Yields: 40

Ingredients

- 1 can of tuna in water undrained
- 1 cup coconut flour
- 1 egg, whisked

Instructions

Set the oven to 350.

Combine the tuna with liquid with the whisked egg. Use a hand blender to puree it.

Add the flour and mix to shape the dough.

Sprinkle the working surface with flour and roll out the dough.

Cut out with small cookie cutters to your liking.

Arrange a sheet pan with baking paper and place the biscuits. Bake for 20 minutes and allow them cool after removing.

Nutritional cat biscuits

While cats can consume a wide choice of foods, it is essential to avoid seasonings and salt in store-bought food. Offer your car the healthy nutrients it needs with this simple salmon biscuit recipe.

Time: 20 minutes

Yields: 40

Ingredients

- 1 (3.5 oz) can salmon undrained
- 3/4 cup all-purpose flour
- 1 large egg

Instructions

Set the oven to 350.

Add the tuna, flour, and egg to a food processor. Pulse until smooth.

Line a sheet with baking paper and spread the mixture into an 8x8 soiree. Pop the biscuits in the oven and bake for 15 minutes.

Let the cat biscuit dough cool a little and cut into ¼ inch squares.

Parmesan cat biscuits

Cheddar and parmesan are some of the approved cheese options suitable for a cat's diet. Prepare these cat biscuits and store them for up to two weeks.

Time: 1 hour 10 minutes

Yields: 50

Ingredients

- 1/2 cup old fashioned oats
- 2 cups all-purpose flour
- 1/4 cup parmesan cheese, grated
- 1/3 cup sharp cheddar cheese, shredded
- 1/3 cup applesauce unsweetened
- 2 tablespoons olive oil
- 3 tablespoons water

Instructions

Set the oven to 350.

Combine the cut biscuit ingredients in a bowl. Form the dough and roll it between two sheets of baking paper to ¼ inch thickness. Adjust with more flour or water if necessary.

Cut out with small cookie cutters to your liking. Arrange a sheet pan with baking paper and place the biscuits. Bake for 20 minutes and let the cat treats cool after removing.

Apple sauce cat biscuits

This is a fantastic combination of sweet potato and apple sauce for your kitty. When using store-bought applesauce, make sure to pick an unsweetened option.

Time: 50 minutes

Yields: 30

Ingredients

- 2 1/2 cups whole wheat flour
- 1/4 cup apple sauce unsweetened
- 1 cup mashed sweet potato

Instructions

Set the oven to 350.

Combine the biscuit ingredients in a mixing bowl. Sprinkle the working surface with flour and roll out the dough to half-inch thickness.

Cut out with small cookie cutters to your liking.

Arrange a sheet pan with baking paper and place the biscuits. Bake for 30 to 40minutes or until browned and let them cool after removing.

Bacon Cat treats

The bacon cat biscuits are a real delicacy, enhanced with cheddar cheese. They love these two ingredients, so give them the treats in moderate amounts.

Time: 40 minutes

Yields: 24

Ingredients

- 2 ½ cups whole wheat flour
- 1 teaspoon Beef Bouillon granules
- 1 large egg
- 1/4 cup chopped bacon
- ½ cup hot water
- 1/4 cup cheddar cheese

Instructions

Set the oven to 350.

Mix the hot water with bouillon to dissolve it. Add flour, bacon, cheese, and egg. Mix and knead into a dough.

Flour the working surface and flatten out the dough.

Cut out with small cookie cutters to your liking.

Arrange a sheet pan with baking paper and place the biscuits. Bake for 25 minutes and let them cool after removing.

Birthday cat treat

If you want to mark your cat's birthday, this is a good recipe. The fish and cheese birthday snack is a great treat once in the year.

Time: 30 minutes

Yields: 2

Ingredients

- 3/4 can salmon
- 3 tablespoons flour
- 3 tablespoons shredded cheese
- 1 egg

Instructions

Set the oven to 350.

Add the salmon into bowls and break it down with a fork. Add the other biscuit ingredients and mix well.

Grease a muffin pan. Transfer to two cups and bake for 20 minutes. Let it cool down completely before serving.

Cheese cat biscuits

The cheese biscuits are a tasty delicacy for your feline friend. The oats will tie the mixture together, so you can pop it in a silicone mold and create perfect shapes.

Time: 10 minutes

Yields: 12

Ingredients

- 2 cups old fashioned oats
- 1 cup shredded cheddar cheese
- 2 eggs
- 3 tablespoons of refined coconut oil

Instructions

Set the oven to 350.

Bring the oats to a food processor and grind them into flour.

Add oil, cheddar, and eggs. Pulse for a minute to combine.

Transfer into a silicone baking sheet and press gently. Bake for 20 minutes and let them cool after removing.

Chicken yogurt cat biscuits

The chicken yogurt biscuits have healthy nutrients and the right amount of protein. The balanced ingredients and the easy preparation process are the main reasons why this recipe will become your fave for cat food.

Time: 40 minutes

Yields: 30

Ingredients

- 1½ cups of boneless chicken meat
- 1 teaspoon of sunflower oil
- 1 tablespoon of yogurt
- 1 egg
- 1 cup rice flour

Instructions

Set the oven to 350.

Chop the meat into chunks and boil it. Let it cool down and use a hand blender to blend it.

Add the yogurt, oil, and egg. Mix well until combined. Add the rice gradually while mixing until dough forms.

Scoop out the biscuits with a teaspoon and flatten them with a fork. Arrange a sheet pan with baking paper and place the biscuits. Bake the treats for 20 minutes and let them cool after removing.

Tuna oat cat biscuits

We know that cats love to eat tuna. Vets recommend tuna in moderate amounts, so giving it as a treat is a good option.

Time: 40 minutes

Yields: 30

Ingredients

- 140 grams of canned tuna, drained
- 1 tablespoon of sunflower oil
- 120 grams of oatmeal
- 1 egg
- 2 tablespoons of water

Instructions

Set the oven to 350.

Combine the oil, egg, and tuna. Add water and oatmeal, constantly stirring until dough forms.

Shape into tiny balls. Arrange a sheet pan with baking paper and place the biscuits. Bake for 15 minutes and let them cool after removing.

Cat biscuits from cat food

If your cat is on a special regime, but you still want to give it a treat, this recipe is for you. It will show you how to prepare tasty treats using dry cat food.

Time: 35 minutes

Yields: 20

Ingredients

- 2 cups cat food dry
- 1 ¼ cups water

Instructions

Add the dry cat food to a blender. Grind it into fine flour.

Transfer the flour to a bowl. Add one cup of water and mix. If the cat food mixture looks too dry, add the remaining ¼ gradually until you reach a nice consistency.

Shape the biscuit mixture into small balls and flatten them with a spoon. Bake for half an hour and cool before serving.

Budget cat biscuits

Every cat loves to munch on treats. When store-bought treats seem too expensive, you can switch them with this option instead.

Time: 25 minutes

Yields: 20

Ingredients

- 6 oz salmon, undrained
- 1 cup flour
- 1 cup cornmeal
- 1/3 cup of water

Instructions

Set the oven to 350.

Combine all cat biscuit ingredients in a mixing bowl. Flour the working surface and flatten out the dough to ¼ inch thick.

Arrange a sheet pan with baking paper and place the biscuits. Bake the treats for 20 minutes and let them cool after removing. Chop to bite-sized pieces.

Turkey cat biscuits

Here we have another pretty simple ca biscuit recipe with only four ingredients. The flour and turkey meat combine to create a tasty treat for your furry friends.

Time: 30 minutes

Yields: 20

Ingredients

- 1/2 cup whole wheat flour
- 1/2 cup ground turkey
- 1/2 tablespoon olive oil
- 1 egg

Instructions

Set the oven to 350.

Combine the cat biscuit ingredients into a mixing bowl.

Flour the working surface and spread out the dough.

Cut out with small cookie cutters to your liking.

Arrange a sheet pan with baking paper and place the biscuits. Bake for 20 minutes and let them cool after removing.

Easy home cooked cat biscuits

If you have more than one cat meowing for treats, this is an ideal recipe that will suit your needs. It yields around 85 pieces, depending on how large you cut them. You will have an enormous batch of homemade treats ready to feed to your kitties at any time. This won't only save you money but also provide your kitties with nutritious bites.

Time: 30 minutes

Yields: 85

Ingredients

- 1 can of tuna in oil
- ¾ cup coconut flour
- ½ cup whole wheat flour
- 1 egg

Instructions

Add the egg and tuna to a food processor. Process to combine.

Transfer to a bowl and add coconut flour and whole wheat flour. Mix to combine.

Knead the dough. It might appear too dry because of the coconut flour, so gradually add up to ⅓ cup water to adjust.

Set the oven to 330.

Flour the working surface and flatten out the dough to a quarter-inch thickness.

Cut out with small cookie cutters to your liking.

Arrange a sheet pan with baking paper and place the biscuits. Bake for 15 minutes and let them cool after removing.

Conclusion

Now when you have the easy cat biscuit recipes, you can prepare healthy treats for your pet. With a simple and quick cooking process, you won't need to spend your time going to the pet store. You will always have healthy treats ready for your cat to enjoy them.

It isn't all about spoiling your cat and providing gourmet treats. Cats with specific food allergies or intolerance will benefit from these recipes. With carefully chosen ingredients, you can prepare treats that promote their health and wellbeing. In addition, your cat will love your homemade biscuits. You won't have to look for other cat food recipes since you already have the best selection in this recipe book.

If you find this recipe book helpful, don't mind checking the other pieces in our collection. You will find complimentary recipe books that match your specific needs!

About the Author

A native of Indianapolis, Indiana, Valeria Ray found her passion for cooking while she was studying English Literature at Oakland City University. She decided to try a cooking course with her friends and the experience changed her forever. She enrolled at the Art Institute of Indiana which offered extensive courses in the culinary Arts. Once Ray dipped her toe in the cooking world, she never looked back.

When Valeria graduated, she worked in French restaurants in the Indianapolis area until she became the head chef at one of the 5-star establishments in the area. Valeria's attention to taste and visual detail caught the eye of a local business person who expressed an interest in publishing her recipes. Valeria began her secondary career authoring cookbooks and e-books which she tackled with as much talent and gusto as her first career. Her passion for food leaps off the page of her books which have colourful anecdotes and stunning pictures of dishes she has prepared herself.

Valeria Ray lives in Indianapolis with her husband of 15 years, Tom, her daughter, Isobel and their loveable Golden Retriever, Goldy. Valeria enjoys cooking special dishes in her large, comfortable kitchen where the family gets involved in preparing meals. This successful, dynamic chef is an inspiration to culinary students and novice cooks everywhere.

Author's Afterthoughts

Thank you for Purchasing my book and taking the time to read it from front to back. I am always grateful when a reader chooses my work and I hope you enjoyed it!

With the vast selection available online, I am touched that you chose to be purchasing my work and take valuable time out of your life to read it. My hope is that you feel you made the right decision.

I very much would like to know what you thought of the book. Please take the time to write an honest and informative review on Amazon.com. Your experience and opinions will be of great benefit to me and those readers looking to make an informed choice.

With much thanks,

Valeria Ray

Printed in Great Britain
by Amazon